# Recharting

## My Way Back

S. Walker

BookLeaf Publishing

India | USA | UK

Made with ❤ on the BookLeaf Publishing Platform

www.bookleafpub.in

www.bookleafpub.com

# Dedication

For my mother, who traced the constellations of our family's story with her hands and heart. She was the cartographer of my childhood, marking each journey with love, each milestone with wisdom. Now, I navigate by the stars she taught me to read, though the maps she left remain unfinished, it is a reminder that even in absence, she guides me still. And for my father, who walked these paths beside us. In memory, in gratitude, in love. We will always be connected.

# Preface

Before my mother died, she was my memory keeper, my compass, my true north. Before my father died, he was my navigator, teaching me to read landscapes both physical and emotional. When we lose our parents, we lose not only the people who loved us first, but also our most reliable witnesses, our primary cartographers, the ones who could verify or correct our remembered coordinates.

This collection began as an attempt to map my way through the first year after their deaths—my father in January, my mother in November, nineteen and six days that redefined my understanding of time and loss. But as I wrote, I discovered that grief follows no linear path, respects no boundaries. It moves like water, like weather, finding its way into every crack and crevice of daily life.

These poems trace multiple geographies: the Missouri of my childhood, my father's Texas roots, the small radius between their house on the hill and mine seven doors down, the institutional corridors of nursing homes, the intimate territory of shared art projects and card games during quarantine. They explore how music becomes a séance, how photographs become portals, how pressed flowers and amateur art become sacred artifacts.

Some of these maps are inherited—my father's way of reading landscapes, my mother's careful cataloging of family stories. Others I've had to draw myself, finding new ways to navigate a world where my primary reference points have vanished. Here are maps of memory and loss, of love and inheritance, of the ways we carry our parents in our bones and blood and gestures.

This is not a complete atlas. There are still blank spaces, territories I haven't found words for yet, coordinates I'm still trying to plot. But perhaps that's fitting—after all, the most honest maps are the unfinished ones, the ones that admit there are places we haven't reached yet, pathways we're still discovering, legends we're still learning to read.

These poems are for anyone who has lost their first cartographers, who is learning to navigate by new stars, who carries maps of love and loss in their DNA. They are for those who understand that every relationship creates its own geography, and that even after our loved ones are gone, we continue to explore and map the territories they left us.

Welcome to this atlas of aftermath, this cartography of continuing.

# Acknowledgements

I am going to keep it simple:

To my mother and father, who gave me my first maps—
of memory, of language, of love.

To Kent, my husband, who helped me navigate the
hardest days, and to our son Adam, who reminds me
daily that love creates its own coordinates.

To Mom and Dad:
every poem is a way of finding my way back to you.

# 1. My Mother's Map

My mother kept directions in her throat—
turn left at the Kennett airport, right
near the Delta Fair grounds, past
the place they tore down, near
the drive-in theater—the empty field.

Her mind was lined with the tributaries
of memory, each story a contour—
a line marking depth. Now I navigate
by absence, consulting blank spaces
on the map where her voice should be.

Each intersection a question I
can't ask—which way led to her
childhood. What landmarks guided her
through the dark? The roads still
ribbon out from town like veins
from a beating heart, but I've lost
my true north, my cardinal reference.

Some days I catch myself speaking
in her cadence, my hands moving
through air like hers did, conducting
an orchestra of remembered streets.

I fold and unfold this emptiness, trying
to make sense of the creases, these
new coordinates of grief. My inheritance—
an atlas of ghost towns, dog-eared pages,
routes that end in middle distance,
trails that fade to white space at the edges.

# 2. Phrenology of Inheritance

My mother's skull was a museum
of borrowed light. Each ridge and hollow
mapped with Victorian precision—here lies music
here mathematics
here the stubborn geography of hope.
I trace my own topography of bone,
searching for her features beneath
my skin—a high sweep, temporal ridge where memory
lives, the occipital curve that holds all childhood songs.

Did she pass down more
than the arch of cheekbone, the particular way
my forehead slopes toward evening? Sometimes
I catch myself humming her songs in the shower,
my fingers finding the same tender spot
above my left ear where she'd press to ease my ache.

Science says these bumps and valleys
mean nothing—no map of soul carved
in calcium, no blueprint of who we are
or were. But still I read my skull like braille,
each depression a letter in an alphabet
of loss, each prominence a word she left behind.

# 3. Winter Cartography

ice builds its own
language

here where water forgets
to be water

(the lake     a white page     spreading north)

each pressure ridge          a new alphabet
of frost

morning:
the sun maps temporary countries
across the freeze

shoreline birds print
their own          desperate
geographies

I trace          the lake's          winter grammar:

white     on     white

on

white

(my father        taught me        to read ice

before books)

now    these crystalline

coordinates

decode        something
about        loss

how        absence        writes itself

in negative space

# 4. November, Lake Huron

The lake knows how to speak in tongues of foam and fury, each wave a different shade of grief. Gray water breaks against gray sky until the boundary blurs. Watch how the lighthouse tries and fails to organize this chaos into something we can navigate by. Its beam cuts through storm-spray like a lost translation, searching for a shore that moved in the night. When they were alive, my parents taught me how to read water-—its moods, its whispers, the way November storms would roll in from Canada like declarations of war. Now, I stand at the edge of this familiar violence, searching for their voices in the wind's anthology of loss. The lake remembers everything: each drowning, every storm-wrecked ship, all the prayers sent out across its waters like paper boats, dissolving in the rain. It holds these stories in its depth, a library of salt and sorrow, catalogued by current, archived in undertow. Tonight the waves speak in my mother's consonants, my father's vowels—a language I almost understand, almost remember, almost forget.

# 5. Her Herbarium of Days

Between pages of Webster's Unabridged, mother
                    pressed time flat—


violet from my first spring dance
Queen Anne's lace from that July picnic
baby's breath from my wedding


Each bloom a bookmark holding open
a door between now & then


Found today—her Wildflowers of the Great Lakes
                thick with ghosted petals
                tissue-thin measurements of love


Rose petal at "perennial"
wild geranium beside "hardy"
forget-me-nots scattered through the index
                            like blue stars


Some flowers have waited so long they've left
their colors on the page, staining paper
                    with their last
                    attempt at bloom

Others crumble at first touch,
become dust of her careful catalogue

She taught me this—
        how to spread each petal wide
        how to arrange the stem just so
        how to close the heavy book & wait

How to label each specimen
        with location
        with date
        with occasion

Latin names like incantations:

Viola sororia   (backyard, Mother's Day)
Lobelia cardinalis   (lake path, August)
Anemone canadensis   (morning you left)

Now I press my own flowers,
place them between pages of her old journals,
letting her handwriting hold them

Two kinds of preservation—
        her words
        these petals

both turning sepia with time
both telling stories of what bloomed
                    of what was gathered
                    of what was saved

# 6. My Border Map

In summer heat that bent the highway lines
      we'd drive south to where
my father's childhood still grew wild in Texas

His Spanish would thicken like honey
      the closer we got,words I half-understood
      blooming in the car's humid air

Grandma's house—a compass point
        fixed in memory's mesquite trees

Her kitchen, where time dissolved
      in steam from frijoles
      tortillas rising like full moons
      her hands teaching mine to pat and turn
      to feel the ancient rhythm of pat-pat-flip
          pat-pat-flip

My father's voice changed there
became music borrowed from his youth—
rolled rs like summer thunder
consonants soft as August dust

I watched him slip back into himself

the self that came before my birth
before the North claimed him

His laugh grew deeper, scattered
with his sister's and brother's voices
        sweet as pecans falling
                in the yard

Now, I trace his journey on maps—
        each borderland where language shifts like sand
        each place his accent changed its mind
        the precise latitude where he learned
                to translate himself

I carry in my blood this mixed geography—
        half mesquite,
        half Michigan pine
        inheritance mapped in the space
                between languages

What migrates—
        recipe cards in two tongues
        proverbs that switch tracks mid-wisdom
        the way his hands moved when he told stories
                of home
                —both homes—

the way mine move now
        speaking in his gestures
        drawing borders in air
        that I'm still learning
        how to cross

# 7. Seven Houses Down

The maps of grief are drawn
in U-turns, in the muscle memory
of avoiding what was once
the straightest path home. Their house
still stands on the hill, lighthouse
of my childhood, but I've learned
to navigate by absence, to read
the braille of empty driveways,
to measure distance in what's lost.

Seven houses-—the space between
who I was and who I am, between
their porch light burning and their
porch light dark. Each mailbox
a waypoint in this geography of sorrow.

One—where mom's roses once grew.
Two—the neighbor, where my dad mowed the yard.
Three—where I learned to ride a bike.
Four—where dad would wave from his work van.
Five—when I knew I went to far from home.
Six—how far mom's voice carried.
Seven—where my new coordinates are alone.

My car knows the detour before I do,
turns right when it should go straight, finds
alternate routes through subdivisions
where no memories live. But some nights,
muscle and bone remember the way up
the hill, past the dip in the road where
rain washes down the yard, toward
the window where their shapes should be,
still telling me to drive safe, call when
I get home, though I'm already here, though
I never really left, though seven houses
might as well be seven thousand miles
of unnavigable darkness between then and now.

Strange how a childhood home
becomes a monument to itself, how
a street can feel like a museum
of discontinued time. Their house still
wears the same paint, holds the same
angle to the sun, catches evening light
like it did when they were just up the hill,
just around the corner,
just a short walk away, just—

# 8. Navigating Green

Between the fog in his mind
        one summer afternoon
                broke through—

my father, who had forgotten
    the names of trees
    of streets
    of me

turned his face toward the window
    and said green,
    so green   today

Three words—a lighthouse beam
    cutting through the murk
    of Lewy bodies, those microscopic thieves
    that stole him piece by piece
        synapse by synapse

The disease had its own topography:
    territories lost and found
    blanks where memories should be
    paths that led to nowhere
    neural networks tangled like kudzu

But for that moment—
        his navigator's eye still true
        still reading the landscape
        like he taught me—


notice   how the sycamores gather light
notice   how summer fills in winter's negative space
notice   how even in Missouri
                something Texas lives
                in the way he sees color
                names it
                holds it in his mouth
                        like a prayer


I drove slower then,
        letting each shade of green last—
                the bright energy of leaves
                the deep emerald of oak
                the forest-tint of maple and persimmon


I watched him and the world remember itself


and for eight blocks,   maybe ten,
        I had my father back—


the one who taught me

to read maps
to measure distance
to find my way home
    by landmarks—

    this oak
    that hill
    the way light moves
    through leaves
    like time through memory

    green
    into gold
    into green
    again

# 9. Return to Michigan

I unearthed them like a bone digger would—
soft cut fossils of being fifteen came
back to my mother—a plaid skirt
a homemade heart zipper
dad's small frame pressed into a wool jacket.

I felt where my mother flooded her reedy body,
her oncewaist trapped in the grip of my fingers.
I held her shape up to see how it looked
open, long, unfolded. I was an explorer—
I wanted her history, her geography to be mine.

I want to take you here, she said
as she held my hand in hers. You
can make it a keepsake. I pocketed
that moment into my dad's letterman
where long passed love letters hid
pencil pressed hearts—
where cold lakelet hands held warmth
in Michigan— where wind moved
their currents together, fixed and set.

And now, here we are on the Black River
footbridge, the longest in Michigan, and I

want to be her for a moment at fifteen—
to be new, to be in love, to hear—twisting
in the wire ropes, inch-thick and root-rusty. I
want to hold on to those side wires
for the first time as she did. To lean over
and breathe in Michigan. I

want to jump—to see the bridge
bounce almost touch the water. I
want to swing from side-to-side and feel
the suspense of being untethered, of being
daughter and mother at once, time folding
like a map of rivers we've crossed. Each
crease holds a story—here, where the paper
wore thin, my mother first kissed my father
beneath cathedral pines. Here, in this fold
she braided my hair the same way her mother did,
fingers mapping familiar paths. Below us,
the Black River writes its own memoir in silt
and stone. I trace its course like a fortune line
on my mother's palm, reading
the future backwards—how I'd stand in
her footsteps, lean into her lean, inherit her
vertigo, her fear of heights, her way of testing
the strength of things that hold us. This

is how we measure time in Michigan—by

bridges crossed, by rivers known, by clothes
kept soft in cedar chests, by stories
passed like silver, tarnished
with each telling. Mother,
let me be fifteen with you. Let me
feel the bridge shudder and hold, let me
learn again how to trust what sways
but doesn't break, how to read
the river's ancient manuscript, how to wear
your youth like a borrowed sweater, warm
with the scent of all our seasons.

# 10. Atlas of Grief

Today I am mapping grief's weather
patterns—how denial arrives like morning
fog over the Missouri
        River, thick
enough to erase the bluffs I know
are there. By noon, anger burns
it off, leaves me standing in the clear
light of what is missing.

I bargain with the mail
carrier—tell him their house is just
up the hill, seven doors
north, where the driveway curves
like a question mark. I have letters for
them—all the stories I keep
saving, all the words I forgot
to say.

Depression is a map maker who
keeps redrawing the boundaries of what
I can bear. Some days it claims whole
territories—the grocery store where mom
bought bananas, dad's favorite
movie theater, the Mexican

restaurant where his Spanish would
bloom like dogwood in spring.

Acceptance comes and
goes like Missouri
seasons—here, then
not here. Today, I found myself
again with mom's songs in the
shower, and for three minutes it felt
right, felt possible to hold both her
absence and her music in the same
breath.

But tomorrow I'll wake to find my
coordinates scrambled—
denial at breakfast, anger with
coffee, bargaining through lunch, depression
settling in with the evening
at home with my son, acceptance just
a theory like lightning
bugs in June—sometimes
visible, mostly
not.

This is my atlas now—each
day a new projection of
loss, each hour a different

scale of missing. The legend
changes constantly—today's acceptance
tomorrow's denial, grief's
longitude and latitude shifting like sand
bars in the river.

I navigate by new
stars—the porch light I keep
burning, dad's coffee cup in the
cabinet, mom's handwriting in old
cookbooks. Each one a different way
to measure the distance between here
and gone, between memory
and morning, between what was
and what
remains.

Some days I am all five
stages before breakfast, some days one
stage plants its flag and claims
the whole territory. Time is no
longer linear—it moves like water, like
weather, like the way the Missouri re
shapes its banks: end
lessly, end
lessly.

# 11. What Blooms

1.

The notepad was cheap
but beautiful—blue-green
with pink flowers dreaming
across its cover, gold letters
promising NOTES, just notes,
as if any of my mother's words
could ever be "just notes."


2.

Chapter 1, she wrote,
*walked into the bathroom*
as if cataloguing ordinary
miracles, marking
time in cold biscuits
and gravy, no plate needed
when you're recording
the story of leaving yourself.


3.

*My writing isn't very good*
*I'm shaky sometimes,*
her pen confessing what
her voice wouldn't, each letter

like the delicate stems on
the cover, trembling truth—
*life really has some surprises*
*for you doesn't it.*

       *Doesn't it.*

4.
She wrote to me directly,
about eyelash kisses
on tiny toes, how she hated
being the mother who needed
instead of gave. *Remember that!!*
She writes to me. Commands me
to hold this close.
*So goofy,* she writes—her voice
exactly as it always was,
floating up from ruled lines.

5.
*Here's to starting a new chapter*
she declares while something
in her turns the final
page. *I'm still shaky,* and I can see it
in the ink, *inside like holding you in*
*one arm and the other hanging*
*loosely by my side.*

She is wild
between the margins.


6.
Her last lines a promise,
a permission
through all this, *I'll be ok.*
*Ok? You hear me?*


*You hear me?*


The question marks multiply
like heartbeats, like flowers
between what she meant
to write and what she could,
between the mother she was
and the mother who wrote,
*I'm falling through it all*
*but it's all ok.*


7.
I keep the notepad inside
my desk, each letter, word, page
a different kind of falling—
through loss and love that
shakes but holds, holds on

shaky but determined
to leave me something
something to hear her voice in,
saying, *Ok?* saying, *listen,*
saying *I'm still here*
in these unsteady lines,
these imperfect, incomplete chapters,
these eyelash kisses
remembered on paper.

# 12. Now That You're Gone, I Keep Remembering to Ask

Was I really allergic to grapefruit
or just that one summer? Did you name me
at home or the hospital? That trip
to the Gulf—was I four or five when
I lost my shoes in the tide?

The details float away like dandelion
seeds. No one left to catch them.
No one to confirm the color
of my first birthday dress,
or why you chose those curtains
in the kitchen, yellow with small
brown flowers, or was
it the other way around?

I find myself reaching for the phone
to ask—what was the name
of that babysitter who taught me
how to blow a bubble? Why did we stop
going to the lake property? Was dad's
cousin really killed by a snake bite?

You kept my history like others

keep photo albums, each memory
filed and sorted, ready to retrieve—
first words, first steps, the time
I choked on spaghetti, how old,
did dad really hold me
upside down, shake me?

Now when Adam asks
what I was like at his age,
I stumble through answers, aware
of all the gaps where your voice
should be, all the details blur and melt
like photographs left in sun.

Did I really hate purple or pink?
Did I cry when we moved
from Kennett? What was the name
of our neighbor's dog or the cat
I got for Christmas, was I eleven?
Was it third grade or fourth
when I won the story contest?

Some nights I dream you still
keep track, record everything
in one of your notebooks—
the recipe for that Christmas candy,
the story behind my middle name,

the real reason you left California,
all the answers I didn't know
I'd need, all the questions
I wasn't wise enough to ask
while you were still here
still remembering
still knowing
still mine.

# 13. Dollar Store Art

At *The Woodlands*, we waged war
     against institutional beige
     with dollar store markers
     and coloring books
     and premade preformed canvases

We made it special, made it ours
     as if art could claim territory
     from fluorescent lights and disinfectant
     as if orange blossoms could transform
     this sterile space into somewhere
        that belonged to you alone
        somewhere you could pretend
          was home

We spent hours   with colors—
     me, always careful
        with boundaries
        or edges
        or stopping points

     you bleeding wild
        across every line

You loved glitter pens—
        how we laughed when silver sparkles
        fell into your water cup
        and you drank cosmos

Now they hang in my dining room
        not quite straight
        or gallery worthy
        or what anyone would call art

but perfect to me as prehistoric hands
        pressed against cave walls—

        here   where your hand was steady
        here   where it shook
        here   where you stayed in the lines
        here   where you gave up trying
        here   where you said good enough
                and meant both the art
                and everything else
                all the things we couldn't say
                        about time
                        or loss
                        or fear

Those cheap velvet cutouts
        of animals

or national parks
guard Adam when he sleeps

like a copper penny under the threshold
like a lucky stone
like all the talismans we create
        to keep ourselves safe

Some people frame diplomas
            or family photos
        or expensive prints

but I frame the proof of our last collaborations—
        gardens that refuse to wilt
                    or fade
                    or die

        memories that spin with defiance
                    and glory

these pieces of time we made beautiful
            and infinite together

these fragments of you I'll never take down
these walls that hold your hands
        making magnificence from nothing
        making ordinary extraordinary

making every moment into something
that would last
and last
and last

# 14. Summoning Gypsy

In photographs from California, maybe 1965,
your blonde hair falls like summer rain—
all that light caught in motion.

You were small enough to disappear into mist,
creamy skin against his darkness—opposites
drawn together like lightning and clear skies.

> Lightning strikes, maybe once,
> maybe twice   and   there
> > you are—

drive with windows down you sing
about mystic undergrounds about rain
wash everything clean about being
a gypsy before you were my mother.

I was small in the back seat I watch
your hand, a wand slice through wind
your turquoise rings become the compass
points to guide us through thunder.

> This gypsy song is my map now
> each chord progression leads back

to your lightning youth—

I go back through the music
		to your ring beats on the steering wheel
		to your voice through thunder
		to your eyes closed at red lights
		just long enough to feel

Now, when the song plays, I summon you in pieces
the silver bangles on your wrist
the way you'd spin in summer storms
your hand reaches for notes only you could see

		Your thunder only happens when it's raining

until your light fades
until the song ends
until the room goes quiet
except for my breath trying to match
a rhythm you used to know by heart

		The gypsy remains
		and somewhere, you're still
		conducting with one hand,
		still singing about the rain,
		still teaching me how music
		makes ghosts of us all.

# 15. The Stories My Father Won

When the Lewy bodies bloomed
in his brain like strange flowers,
they seeded magnificent dreams—
$168 million in prize money
a guitar duet with Willie Nelson
his name in Oscar lights.

I learned to navigate his new
geographies of joy, these glittering
countries of almost-true. *Yes*, dad,
*Willie called again—*
*he wants to practice your song.*

What harm in letting him believe
his fingers knew guitar strings, that
his voice could carriy a tune? Some
days I'd help him count his millions—
imaginary interest accruing
in imaginary banks, his face
bright and proud and real.

He'd tell me, *I'm saving most of it*
*for you, honey.* And wasn't that the truth,

this inheritance of beautiful delusions?
These stories worth more than money—
my father on stage, my father in Willie's
tour bus trading song verses, my father
rich with more than disease could steal.

I drove him to the bank where
his millions waited. *Closed today*, I'd say,
*They're still counting it all.* Each lie
a small mercy, each fiction a shield against
the harder truth—a blaze of brain misfires.

In later moments, he'd almost
remember—did Willie like my song?
And I'd tell him *yes, god yes, he loved it,*
*you should have seen the smilie, should*
*have heard the crowd cheer.*

Some nights I dream them all
true—the millions materializing
in his account, Willie Nelson waiting
in our driveway, Oscar gold caught
in the sun. In these dreams, his mind
stays clear as spring, his hands
steady on strings, his voice strong,
songs in perfect time, in perfect truth.

I want to live there, in that bright
country of his beautiful beliefs, where
every delusion blooms into fact, where
every story he told writes itself real, where
my father is still rich with dreams I
don't have to pretend to believe, where I
never have to say the bank is closed, *daddy
let's try again tomorrow,* where tomorrow
always comes, shining with promise,
pitch-perfect and true.

# 16. Sequence and Time

Strange to miss a plague year,
                      but I do
Our kitchen table an island
       in the quarantine sea
       Sequence cards dealt like prayers
                      each night
Dad shuffling with rough hands
  mom sorting her cards just so
       while outside the world
        counted its losses
We counted different things
       how many two-eyed jacks
       how many one-eyed jacks
       how many ways to block
       each other's paths across
        that cardboard world
Sweet arithmetic
       three cookies left
       two cups of coffee
       one more game before bed
If I had known the math that waited
       2019
       becoming 2023
       becoming nineteen days into January

                losing my father
        becoming six days into November
                    when mom followed
Numbers I can't stop
        adding
        subtracting
        dividing into grief
But then, we were just placing chips
        on diamonds
        on hearts
        on spades that meant nothing more
                than wins in a game
Dad still knowing which card played when
Mom still keeping score in her head
Time still a thing we thought we had
We were kings and queens
        safe in our bubble
        of not knowing these were
                the last games
Now nineteen and six haunt me
        like wild cards in a game
        I never meant to play
        a sequence I can't complete
Strange to miss a plague
but I'd return there now
Return to—
        that kitchen table

those nights
the careful placement of green chips
                              blue chips
the quiet click of pieces
        falling into place
the time before time became
        a thing I count
        in days without
Deal the cards again
Let's play one more round
Let me have that year back
        that table
        that game
        those hands holding cards
        those voices calling plays
        that perfect sequence of moments
Before numbers
became more than just places
        on a board
became the mathematics
        of goodbye

# 17. New Units of Measurement

Before they died, I thought I knew
what sadness meant—a broken heart
at sixteen, a lost job, a friend's slow
drift away. How naive I was to measure
oceans in teaspoons, call paper cuts catastrophes.

Now I know—grief is its own periodic table
of elements, each loss a new compound
of impossible weight. The day dad forgot home
was home burns at absolute zero. The night
mom stopped breathing splits atoms in my chest.

I used to rate pain on a scale of one
to ten. Now I laugh at that number line—
how innocent, to think pain could be contained
in integers, to think there was a ceiling
to suffering, a maximum capacity to loss.

What I called loneliness before was just
solitude wearing a darker dress. True
loneliness is walking past their house.
I thought I understood anger when
lovers left, when friends betrayed, when

life seemed unfair. But now I know—
that was just practice rage, minor scales
before the symphony of fury that is disease
erase your father neuron by neuron, your
mother's bones and marrow and body
betray her breath by breath.

What metric measures the space between
who I was when they lived and who I am
in this after? How do I calculate
the density of absence
the half-life of memory
the velocity of loss?

They should recalibrate all dictionaries now—
**sad** (adj.): see the empty
chairs at Christmas
**lonely** (adj.): see the questions
that have no one left to answer
**grief** (n.): see how your mother's voice
becomes a stranger
in your own mouth

The old mathematics of emotion fails
me now. Everything before was algebra—
this is quantum physics, theoretical dimensions,
string theory of the heart. I am learning

new equations for survival, new ways to solve
for x where x equals the rest of my life
without them.

This is the advanced calculus of orphan
hood—how every memory derivatives
into loss, how time integrals into forever, how
love multiplies by absence to equal this
infinite ache that redefines all lesser sorrows,
that makes me wish I could reach back through
time and hold that younger me
who thought she understood pain
who had no idea how blessed
she was to be so wrong.

# 18. Ways We Might Meet Again

Maybe the physicists are right
and parallel universes stack
like pages in an infinite book—
somewhere you're still climbing
that hill to your house, somewhere
we're still playing Sequence
during lockdown, somewhere
time branched differently and I
never had to learn the word goodbye.

Or perhaps the Buddhists know—
karma spinning like a wheel,
lives cycling like seasons.
Next time I'll be the mother,
you the daughter, or we'll meet
as sisters, as friends, as two
strangers who feel oddly
familiar in a coffee shop
in some future century.

Could be the quantum theorists
have it—consciousness as light
waves, never dying, just changing

form. Your thoughts and mine
still entangled across space-time,
still influencing each other's
particles, still dancing that atomic
dance of mother, daughter, father,
child—energy neither created
nor destroyed, just transformed.

Maybe the mediums aren't wrong—
you exist now on a different
frequency, like radio waves
I almost catch between stations.
Sometimes I think I hear you
in white noise, in static, in that
split second between sleep
and waking when reality hasn't
quite solidified.

Or it's like string theory suggests—
eleven dimensions folded
into space smaller than atoms.
You're just there, on the other
side of a cosmic membrane,
close as breath, separated only
by the thinnest wall of reality.

Could be the Indigenous peoples

know the truth—you've joined
the ancestors who watch us
from stars, from ravens' wings,
from the spaces between
heartbeats. You're in the wind
that moves through Missouri
trees, in the river's long memory,
in the dirt beneath my feet.

Some say time is a circle,
not a line—future, past,
and present all existing
at once. Which means you're
still there, I'm still here,
we're always at that kitchen
table, always walking that hill,
always saying both hello
and goodbye in the same
eternal moment.

Perhaps the poets are right
and we live on in metaphor,
in memory, in the stories
proteins tell DNA, in the way
my hands move like yours now,
in how your voice becomes
mine when I least expect it.

Or maybe it's simpler—
maybe love is its own
dimension, its own
scientific law, its own
proof of continuation.
Maybe these bonds we forge
in life are quantum-entangled,
karma-proof, god-blessed,
ancestor-strong, time-defying,
universe-spanning things
that even death can't fully
understand or break.

I don't know if I believe
in pearly gates or golden
streets, but I believe in all
these possibilities of you—
wave and particle, spirit
and memory, energy and light,
matter and miracle. I believe
in every theory that says
this separation is temporary,
that love finds ways to cross
dimensions, that somewhere
somehow, in some form
we are still together

we are always together
we will be together again

# 19. 198 Miles South

The GPS says three hours to Kennett—
past farmland, past river towns,
past the gradual flattening of Missouri
into delta soil and cotton. They rest there now,
among aunts and uncles, grandparents,
all those voices now silent under stones.

198 miles between my coffee cup
and their granite markers. Too far
to visit on lunch breaks, too far
 or quick hellos, too far for all
these daily things I need to tell you:
Mom, Adam was amazing in hockey today.

He wants to be, in this order:
  an astronaut
  a professional fisherman
  maybe something with computers
   or art or bugs
  and if all else fails,
  there's always Culvers

You'd laugh at that last part,
add it to your collection of grandson

stories, tell me again about that bass
you caught in '86, the one that still hangs
in our basement like it hung in yours,
a legacy of luck and patience Adam
studies now, asking questions
only you can answer.

I want to drive through Starbucks,
order your lemon loaf, your light roast,
carry them three minutes up the hill
instead of three hours south. I want
to sit at your table, watch you make
lists of Adam's possibilities, hear you
say see how far he'll go while I nod,
knowing how far now means something
different, means Kennett's clay soil,
means distance I can't cross
with a short drive, means every mile
between here and there is measured
in things I can't tell you:
        his growing height
        his voice changing
        his questions about fishing
        his dreams of space
        all these stories
        that end in silence
        198 miles away

The bass still watches from its wooden frame,
its glass eyes holding secrets
of summer lakes, of your skill,
of stories Adam will never hear
in your voice. But he asks,
and I tell him what I know:
how you cast your line just so,
how patience runs in our blood,
how some distances can only be measured
in memories, in missed conversations,
in coffee that stay too long
on counters, growing cold.

# 20. Wearing Time, Notes on Paul Sebastian

In 1979, they bottled time—
lavender lifting from skin like morning
sage speaking in his nutmeg memories
I spray his cologne on wrists now,
      where pulse meets air,
      where blood keeps time
Each note a coordinate of him—

ylang-ylang, the way he'd lean to kiss mom goodbye
rose, his hands repairing appliances
jasmine, summer in the back yard
cloves, how he measured life
never needing cups or spoons

Some mornings I find his bottle
      nearly empty—wonder if scent
      can evaporate like memory,
      if molecules grow tired
      of holding shape
I carry him in chemistry, in suspended
      spice and flower—
      this spell bottled in glass
Oakmoss grounds him in my present:

walking into rooms
he never saw, leaving traces
of him in air that never
knew his breath
Sometimes strangers catch his scent—
turn their heads as if they too
remember something lost,
something preserved amber
in its resin trap
like prehistoric insects
Musk remembers his skin:
how mortality smells sealed
in crystal and memory
Each application a ritual now—
remove cap
hold bottle
(remember)
(invoke)
(return)
This is how we keep
the dead with us—
I map him on my body—
right wrist:1979
left wrist: 2023
collar bone: where his hugs landed
chest: where my loss lives
Some nights I dream in Paul Sebastian—

his molecules replacing mine,
his atoms building roads like poems,
like proof that somewhere
he still breathes

# 21. Their Time Keeps Living Here

From its post between window and door,
our grandfather clock stands sentinel—
all-seeing eye, brass-hearted guardian,
oldest witness to what endures

It guards the threshold, an ancient deity, marking
who enters, who leaves, who returns, who stays—
keeping inventory of our breathing

Eight feet tall in carved mahogany, it maps
each hour with sailors' precision—tiny ships
forever tacking across the dome of its face

Up there, painted waves never crest, sails
never furl, those miniature crews forever bound
for harbors they'll never reach

The sound depends on time of day—
    midnight brings whale-deep bells
    morning chimes like church hymns
    afternoon rings lighter
    twilight tolls like memory

It keeps their stories behind glass—each tick
a syllable each tock a sentence each hour
a chapter in the book of our continuing

It remembers everything— how they moved
through these rooms, how we move through
them now, translating loss and love

Every Sunday I perform the ritual—hold key warm
from waiting crank full turns for the weights
two quarter-turns for the chime like combination
numbers to a safe that holds their remaining time

Behind glass, the lyre strings stand sentinel—
Adam's growth marked in inches
Kent's morning coffee
my pauses between tasks to watch
the pendulum swing

It witnesses our daily liturgy— breakfast dishes
and homework and cats and play and dinner
The ships above keep their compass true while
below, brass weights descend like sun
and moon and stars, measuring days in gravity and gold

Their anniversary plate—twenty-four years caught
in metal, now carried forward by this time-keeper, this

brass-hearted house, this guardian of their hours

It sees everything—front door open, side door close
cats stretch in squares of morning light, life move
through rooms they'll never visit again

It holds the border og now and then, here and
gone, between what we've lost and
what remains—alert as my mother's
ear, constant as my father's love

It counts heartbeats we can't hear, marks
time in their absence—tick for mother's laugh
tock for father's sigh tick for every moment
                         tock for every moment

Some nights I catch it glowing, face bright
as a full moon, watching over our sleep— steady
as a pulse, faithful as a promise, turning time
into music, absence into presence, house into home

www.ingramcontent.com/pod-product-compliance
Lightning Source LLC
LaVergne TN
LVHW021233200726
843509LV00012B/1480